apple

P9-CDW-303

MONSTERS & MYTHS
ANCIENT LEGENDS

By Gerrie McCall and Lisa Regan

Gareth Stevens
Publishing

Please visit our Web site, www.garethstevens.com. For a free color catalog of all our high-quality books, call toll free 1-800-542-2595 or fax 1-877-542-2596.

Library of Congress Cataloging-in-Publication Data

McCall, Gerrie.
  Ancient legends / Gerrie McCall and Lisa Regan.
      p. cm.
  ISBN 978-1-4339-4988-3 (library binding)
  ISBN 978-1-4339-4989-0 (pbk.)
  ISBN 978-1-4339-4990-6 (6-pack)
  1. Animals, Mythical. 2. Monsters. I. Regan, Lisa, 1971- II. Title. III. Title: Monsters and myths.
  GR825.M26 2011
  398.24'54–dc22
                                    2010039131

Published in 2011 by
Gareth Stevens Publishing
111 East 14th Street, Suite 349
New York, NY 10003

Printed in the United States of America

CPSIA compliance information: Batch #CW11GS: For further information contact Gareth Stevens, New York, New York at 1-800-542-2595.

Table of Contents

Baba Yaga

FACE
Her hideous face has a hooked nose and eyes that can turn her victims to stone just by looking at them.

BODY
She has a huge, cannibalistic appetite but still remains extremely thin, with bony legs like a skeleton's legs.

SIZE
Baba Yaga is so huge that when she lies down in her hut, her nose touches the ceiling and her feet and head touch the walls.

MOUTH
Her mouth is as big as a cave, and she can swallow people whole. Her teeth are like knife blades and may be made of iron or stone.

In some stories, Baba Yaga is an old woman or a beautiful lady who gives out gifts and help, but in many tales she is a wicked old crone who eats children. She flies through the air in a mortar or iron kettle, using the pestle or her broom to propel her along and sweep away her tracks in the air so that no one can follow her. She is often assisted by three pairs of hands, with no body, that appear from thin air to perform tasks for her. She has a huge oven for cooking children and sleeps on it at night to keep warm.

Baba Yaga lives deep in the forest in a most peculiar, and unnerving, home. Her house is a hut that stands on large chicken legs and is surrounded by a fence of human bones. These are the bones of her victims. The hut is constantly on the move, screeching and spinning on its fowl legs in a clearing in the middle of the trees. If anyone dares to come close, the hut spins around to stay turned away from the visitor.

ACTUAL SIZE

WHERE IN THE WORLD?

RUSSIA

EASTERN EUROPE

Children all around eastern Europe and across Russia know the tales of Baba Yaga and her scary hen-leg hut.

DID YOU KNOW?

• Some tales tell of three horsemen who ride out each day from Baba Yaga's hut. The first is all white and is the dawn. The second is red, for the brightness of the daytime sun. The third is as black as the night he represents.

• Sometimes the stories include her sisters who are as frightening and horrible as she is. They are all called Baba Yaga, just to confuse things!

• Baba Yaga has no power over people who are good and pure or those who are protected by a parent's love. One Russian fairy story tells of Vasilisa, a young and sweet girl, who has to perform tasks in Baba Yaga's hut and is protected by her mother's blessing.

Banshee

EYES
Look out for a banshee's eyes! They are red from crying, and usually brimming with more tears, ready to fall.

HAIR
A banshee's long hair flows down her back. Often gray or a dull brown in color, it is ragged and knotted.

VOICE
A banshee's wail is a sound you never want to hear. It combines the worst elements of a baby's cries, a wolf's call, and the mournful winds of death.

AGE
Young and beautiful or old and haggard? Banshees take on both forms but always bring the same sorrow.

CLOTHING
Watch out for a woman in a long, gray cloak with a hood—she may be on the prowl for death. Some banshees wear death robes underneath their cloaks, while others wear a long, green dress.

Widely known as bearers of bad news, banshees are female fairies—but not in the pretty, dainty form known from childhood fairy tales. Instead, these spirits can be haggard and grim, and always mean that a human life is doomed. The appearance of a banshee is an omen of a death. A banshee traditionally "adopts" a family and lets out an agonizing wail when one member is about to die. She begins to weep as if she will never stop crying. Sometimes she can be found washing the blood-stained clothes of the person, just before they pass away.

It is said that the ancient Celtic people, the Tuatha de Danann, were the fairy ancestors of the banshees. After defeat in a battle, they moved underground and lived in grassy mounds. Each group had a fairy heaven, known as "sidhe." The banshees leave these subterranean homes in search of their doomed adoptive family. If several banshees appear at once, it foretells the death of somebody extremely important. A banshee can wail at the death of a family member even if he or she is far away, for example on a crusade or in battle.

ACTUAL SIZE

WHERE IN THE WORLD?

● SCOTLAND

● IRELAND

GREAT BRITAIN

The Celts spread across parts of Great Britain from central Europe. Most banshees attached themselves to Irish or Scottish families.

DID YOU KNOW?

• Legend says that sprinkling oats on yourself, or keeping some in your pocket, can ward off banshees.

• The name "banshee" comes from the Irish "bean sidhe" meaning "woman of the fairy hill."

• Many Irish stories tell of the banshee singing to a dying ancestor to carry his or her soul across to the other world.

• A banshee's wail can be piercing enough to shatter glass and should strike fear into the heart of anyone unlucky enough to hear it.

Black Dog

EYES
Some report eyes glowing with evil. Others tell of terrible, empty black pits.

COAT
Blacker than night, this doesn't gleam in the moonlight like the coat of a living dog.

CLAWS
These spring viciously from huge paws that make no sound as the monster lopes along. The paws also leave no prints, even in the softest soil.

MOUTH
The teeth are hideously long and sharp, and foul saliva reeking of sulfur may drool from the beast's jaws.

Folklore has it that if you see a phantom hound with a black coat and blazing eyes at night, bad luck or even death is close at hand. This huge dog has demonic red eyes, and it appears only at night, terrifying lone travelers. It is said that you will feel an unnatural chill before you see it appear. Tales of black dogs are especially common in Britain, though some experts think Viking raiders brought these stories with them from Scandinavia. The dogs are often linked with churches. A black dog that visited the church of Blythburgh in Suffolk in 1577 killed three people. Black dog stories influenced Arthur Conan Doyle when he wrote his Sherlock Holmes story, *The Hound of the Baskervilles.*

A man walking home one evening took a shortcut along a clifftop path. He didn't believe local stories about a black dog. As he walked, a mist descended and he started to feel cold— unnaturally so. Though uneasy, he pressed on. Suddenly, he came face-to-face with a monstrous, ghostly hound, its eyes burning with an unearthly fire. The man turned and ran in blind panic—and plunged over the cliff, screaming to his death.

WHERE IN THE WORLD?

BRITISH ISLES

EASTERN NORTH AMERICA

EUROPE

Most tales of black dogs come from Britain and Ireland, but there have been sporadic sightings in Scandinavia, Germany, France, and even as far away as Nova Scotia in Canada and the eastern United States.

ACTUAL SIZE

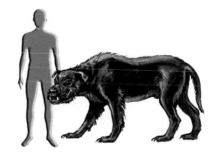

DID YOU KNOW?

• **The earliest known report of a black dog was in France in AD 856, when one materialized in a church even though the doors were shut. The church grew dark as it padded up and down the aisle, as if looking for someone. The dog then vanished as suddenly as it had appeared.**

• **In Missouri, a hunter once threw an ax at an enormous black dog. The ax passed right through the beast's ghostly body.**

European Unicorns

HORN
The European unicorn usually has a pure white horn, but some books and art depict it with a jet-black horn instead.

HAIR
The European unicorn's hair was found in its mane and its tail, although some pictures also show the unicorn with a short, curling beard.

TEETH
The European unicorn was a grazing animal, and had teeth like a horse's that were good for grinding up plant food.

BLOOD
The blood of the European unicorn was thought to have the power to heal if applied to sick or injured people.

The European unicorn is the most popular type seen in movies and books. It is usually a pure white animal about the size of a small horse with an elegant body and prancing walk. Stories about the European unicorn start well back in Roman times, yet it was during the medieval period that the unicorn truly became popular in Europe. The unicorn was used in art to represent purity, or the person of Jesus Christ. Unicorns were also symbols of power and hunting, so they appeared on many official crests and coats of arms.

ACTUAL
SIZE

A man drinks from a precious alicorn. In the medieval imagination, the horn of a unicorn had great magical powers. It could heal the sick, bring longer life, or even be used as a weapon to destroy evil creatures. This man is taking a drink from an alicorn, the life-giving strength of the horn mingling with the wine poured into it. But mortal and immortal things are not meant to touch, and many people who had alicorns found they brought as many curses as blessings.

WHERE IN THE WORLD?

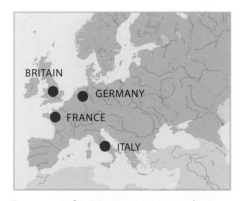

BRITAIN

GERMANY

FRANCE

ITALY

Reports of unicorns seem to have spread from the Greek and Roman world up into western and northern Europe over the course of several hundred years. Germany, France, Italy, and Britain have particularly strong unicorn traditions.

DID YOU KNOW?

• Some medieval European writers wrote that the unicorn could remove poisons from plants or water by making the sign of the Christian cross.

• Between 1550 and 1700, at least 25 books or long chapters in books were devoted entirely to the discussion of unicorns.

• Many churches around Europe were supposed to have pieces of unicorn horn on display. In the monastery of St. Denis near Paris, for example, the priests listed an alicorn among their possessions. It was 7 feet (2 m) long and weighed a total of 7 pounds (3 kg). It was said to have come from a unicorn killed in Persia. This great horn was taken from the monastery in the aftermath of the French Revolution of 1789. The church of St. Mark's in Venice was also famously said to hold two alicorns.

Evil Queen

FACE
Her lovely face is not a true reflection of her jealous and corrupt soul. Being beautiful is not enough for the evil queen, and so she kills innocent Snow White to claim the title of most beautiful.

HANDS
The queen's graceful hands conjure up cruel spells and create poisonous objects.

BODY
The attractive queen uses magic to transform herself into the shape of a lace peddler or a harmless old woman selling apples.

Aproud, beautiful queen with supernatural powers asks her magic mirror the same question each day: "Who is the fairest in the land?" The mirror always replies that the queen is the fairest in the land. One day, though, the mirror responds differently, saying the fairest in the land is Snow White. The jealous queen sends Snow White into the forest with a huntsman. He has orders to kill Snow White and bring back her lungs and liver as proof that she is dead. The huntsman pities Snow White and lets her live. He kills a wild boar and takes its lungs and liver to the queen.

The evil queen eats the lungs and liver, believing they are Snow White's. Seven friendly dwarves take Snow White into their home. The next time the evil queen asks her mirror the daily question, it replies "Snow White," and the queen knows that the girl is still alive. The queen disguises herself as a peddler selling lace. She wraps Snow White so tightly in laces that the girl cannot breathe and faints. The dwarves save Snow White by cutting the laces away. The queen knows that Snow White lives because the mirror still identifies her as the fairest.

ACTUAL SIZE

WHERE IN THE WORLD?

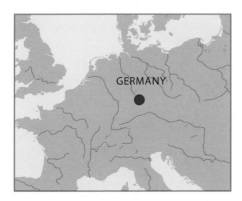

GERMANY

The evil queen holds her grudge against the beautiful Snow White from her castle high up on a hill in Germany.

DID YOU KNOW?

• The evil queen produces a poisoned comb, but the dwarves pull the comb from Snow White's hair and save her. Once again, the mirror's answer that Snow White is the fairest confirms she is alive.

• Using black magic, the vain queen poisons an apple that kills Snow White. The dwarves place Snow White in a glass coffin on a hilltop, where she lies for years but does not decay. A passing prince asks if he may have the beautiful girl in the coffin. When his servants move the coffin, they jostle it and the bite of poisoned apple is jarred loose from Snow White's mouth. Snow White comes back to life.

• The evil queen attends the wedding of Snow White and the prince. A pair of iron slippers is heated in a fire and the evil queen is forced to dance in the red-hot shoes until she drops to the floor, dead.

Fenrir

EARS
Able to hear a twig snap across the continent of Europe, Fenrir's keen hearing grows ever sharper as his body increases to enormous proportions.

LEGS
The long, slender legs are muscular, allowing Fenrir to chase prey for long periods without tiring.

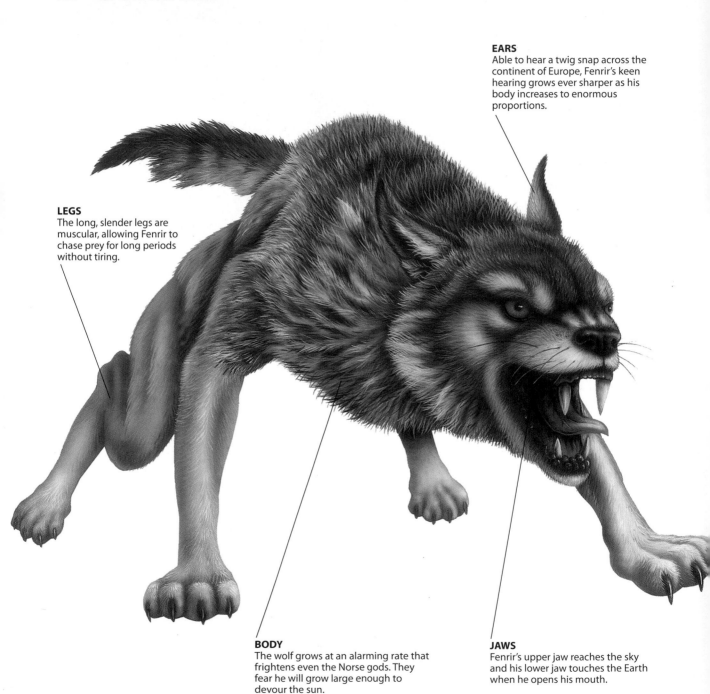

BODY
The wolf grows at an alarming rate that frightens even the Norse gods. They fear he will grow large enough to devour the sun.

JAWS
Fenrir's upper jaw reaches the sky and his lower jaw touches the Earth when he opens his mouth.

A prophecy states that the gigantic wolf Fenrir and his family will one day destroy the world. Even the gods fear Fenrir, the child of a giantess and Loki, the father of all lies. Odin, the chief god in Norse mythology, hopes to tame Fenrir, but all the other gods shrink at the sight of the wolf. Only Tyr, the god of war, is brave enough to feed the rapidly growing beast. The gods bind the hungry wolf with chains, but twice he breaks loose. Elves create a magic ribbon that will hold Fenrir. The powerful wolf does not trust the gods and senses the ribbon may contain magic beyond his powers.

Fenrir insists that one of the gods place a hand in his mouth as a gesture of good faith that no magic will be used against him. Tyr is the only one brave enough to place his hand in the wolf's mouth. When Fenrir realizes he cannot break the magic ribbon, he bites off Tyr's hand. Fenrir fights against his restraints, but the gods prop open his mouth with a sword to keep him from biting. The blood and drool that run from his jaws form a rushing river.

ACTUAL SIZE

WHERE IN THE WORLD?

SCANDINAVIA ●

Fenrir's terrible howls can be heard throughout the Scandinavian countries of Norway, Sweden, and Denmark.

DID YOU KNOW?

• **Fenrir bursts free to take his revenge during the battle at the end of the world. He belches fire and smoke, creating clouds of deadly vapors that fill heaven and Earth with his poisonous breath.**

• **Fenrir defeats Odin by growing larger and larger as they fight. Once Fenrir's jaws embrace all the space between heaven and Earth, he swallows Odin whole.**

• **Odin's son Vidar steps on Fenrir's lower jaw, seizes the wolf's upper jaw in his hands, and rips the dreadful monster in half.**

• **The unbreakable ribbon spun by the elves to hold Fenrir is made of a mountain's roots, a woman's beard, a cat's footsteps, a fish's voice, a bird's spittle, and a bear's sinews.**

Ghoul

BODY
A ghoul has the spindly, weakened body of one that has been dead for a while. Its bones are still covered in graying flesh, but it has no muscle strength.

FACE
A terrifying sight, the ghoul has sunken eyes and a gaping hole for a nose. It is as if a skull has been covered with skin but no meat.

JAWS
Despite the rotting appearance of a ghoul, it has a strong set of jaws and razor-sharp teeth for tearing at the flesh of a corpse.

CLOTHING
Ghouls may be naked, but often wear the last rags of the clothes they wore before they became a ghoul.

Ghouls have changed through the years of storytelling. Originally a shape-shifting demon that preys upon travelers, especially in the wilderness (deserts and lonely forests are their favorites), they hide in caves and wait for humans to pass by. They are grotesque but lust after humans. They often operate after dark to trap or terrorize their victim. They may take on an animal form, such as a hyena, or adopt the legs of a donkey and the horns of a goat. They love the taste of human flesh and are not fussy how old (or dead) it is. They often raid graveyards for a meal.

 The modern ghoul is less imaginative in its form and more gruesome. Usually shown as undead humans with partly rotting flesh, they tear the limbs off human corpses. These modern ghouls are not particularly clever and cower away from healthy humans if confronted. They may gather in gangs to outnumber a human, and are more likely to tackle an old or weakened victim. They hang around graveyards and tombs, raiding coffins to find newly buried bodies to satisfy their hunger. A coffin with its nails removed is a sure sign a ghoul has been at work.

ACTUAL SIZE

WHERE IN THE WORLD?

PERSIA ●
ARABIA ●

The 21st-century ghoul can be found around the world, but the stories originated in ancient Arabian and Persian folklore.

DID YOU KNOW?

• The ghoul of Persian myths is the servant of the evil god Ahriman and is weak-minded and easily led.

• In one form, the ghoul is described as an extremely ugly creature that looks a little like a one-eyed ostrich.

• A person may be described as "ghoulish" if they are strangely and unnaturally obsessed with anything gruesome or linked to death.

• Although ghouls are cannibals, they prefer the aging meat of a dead body to the fresh blood of live prey. In this way, they are different from the zombies of modern horror stories.

• The ancient collection of tales *One Thousand and One Nights* (often called the *Arabian Nights*) features the earliest ghouls in literature. They appear in many modern books, including the Harry Potter stories.

Huitzilopochtli

FACE
Huitzilopochtli's face was the hideous stuff of nightmares. He was painted blue, with oversized teeth and an unforgiving glare.

NAME
His name means "blue hummingbird on the left," and he was shown as a blue-skinned man with a headdress made of hummingbird feathers.

WARRIOR
Although he was a god, Huitzilopochtli was also worshiped as a mighty warrior armed with a round shield and a turquoise snake on his spear.

DAGGER
His dagger is a priest's sacrificial knife, used for carving out the organs of victims to offer up to the gods. It is made of stone, gold, and precious gems.

This mighty god was a bad boy from day one. In Aztec tales, he was born the son of the earth goddess Coatlicue, who became pregnant by placing magical hummingbird feathers in her dress. Her other children did not like this and wanted to kill her. Huitzilopochtli was born already wearing armor and carrying magic weapons, which allowed him to cut off his sister's head and kill many of his hundreds of brothers. These brothers were the moon and the stars, and the sun will always be able to wipe them out with its rays. Huitzilopochtli became the most important and most worshipped of all Aztec gods.

Huitzilopochtli was a hungry god and demanded many sacrifices. His followers usually offered up prisoners taken in their many wars. The unfortunate victim would be pinned down to a sacrificial stone or altar, where the priest would plunge a dagger into his bare chest. The priest ripped out the man's heart and thrust it high in the air for the sun god's approval. If the sun god was kept happy, the people would get the rains they needed for their crops, good harvests, and victory in their wars.

ACTUAL SIZE

WHERE IN THE WORLD?

MEXICO

Huitzilopochtli was the Aztec god of the sun and of war. The Aztecs lived in Mexico from the 14th to the 16th century.

DID YOU KNOW?

• In Aztec legend, Huitzilopochtli led the Aztecs to the Mexico Valley, where they saw an eagle perched on a cactus, eating a snake. This is now a national symbol of Mexico.

• The eagle was seen as a prophetic sign, and Huitzilopochtli persuaded them to stay and live in the area. They built their city of Tenochtitlan, which is now the center of Mexico City.

• A great pyramid was built to honor Huitzilopochtli. It's said that when it was finished, more than 20,000 people were sacrificed in a ceremony there.

• It was believed that the victims of the sacrifices became part of the brilliance of the sun for four years, when their souls were sent into the body of a hummingbird forever afterward.

Mordred

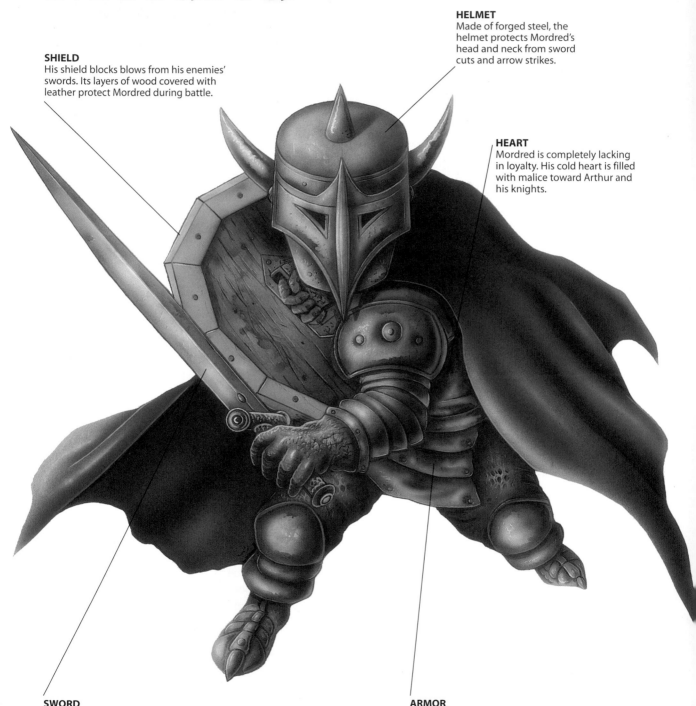

HELMET
Made of forged steel, the helmet protects Mordred's head and neck from sword cuts and arrow strikes.

SHIELD
His shield blocks blows from his enemies' swords. Its layers of wood covered with leather protect Mordred during battle.

HEART
Mordred is completely lacking in loyalty. His cold heart is filled with malice toward Arthur and his knights.

SWORD
He slashes and cuts his way through battle, using the sharp, pointed tip of his sword for thrusting. Mordred uses this sword to fatally wound King Arthur.

ARMOR
Mordred's plate armor is practically sword proof. The only way he can be killed is by a well-aimed sword thrust to a joint, where there is only weaker chain mail to protect him.

Sir Mordred the Traitor is a warrior chief. His betrayals lead first to the downfall of King Arthur and then to the destruction of the Round Table. Mordred is unkind to the younger knights, mocking them publicly. King Arthur is unaware that Queen Guinevere and Sir Lancelot are in love with each other. Mordred exposes them to Arthur and, according to the law, Arthur must now put to death his queen and dearest friend. Lancelot flees, though he returns to rescue Guinevere from being burned at the stake.

ACTUAL SIZE

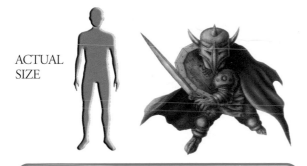

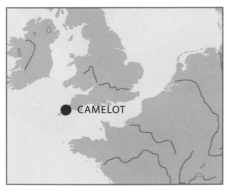

Arthur travels to France to fight Lancelot and makes Mordred his deputy ruler. While Arthur is away, Mordred falsely announces that Arthur is dead. Mordred then seizes the crown and forms an alliance with the Saxons, giving them a hold in Britain in return for their aid and support. Mordred tries to take Guinevere as his wife. She pretends to agree to the arrangement but hides from Mordred in the Tower of London. Guinevere and a loyal garrison withstand a siege by Mordred's troops. Arthur returns to England and battles Mordred. Arthur kills Mordred, but Arthur himself is mortally wounded during combat.

WHERE IN THE WORLD?

CAMELOT

According to Arthurian legend, Sir Mordred betrayed his king and destroyed the fellowship of the Knights of the Round Table in Camelot, allegedly located in Cornwall, England.

DID YOU KNOW?

• **The wizard Merlin predicted that a child born on May Day would kill King Arthur and wipe out his kingdom. To protect himself, Arthur had all children born on May Day gathered up and sent out to sea on a leaky ship. All of the children drowned but one. The lone survivor was Mordred.**

• **Mordred was officially King Arthur's nephew, but there are rumors that he is actually a son that Arthur refused to claim as his own.**

• **Mordred violates every requirement in the knights' code of chivalry, including committing treason, murdering, and engaging in battle over wrongful quarrels.**

ANCIENT LEGENDS

Nuckelavee

HEADS
The horse's head is magnificent, though fearsome, but the human head is grotesquely large on its shoulders.

EYES
Many accounts say that both the human head and the horse's head have only a single, fiery red eye in the center of the forehead. When shown with two eyes each, they are still lit with the fires of hell.

BODY
This gruesome creature has no skin to cover its flesh. Every inch of its body is pulsing muscle, vein, and cartilage visible to everyone.

MOUTH
When either head opens its mouth, it shows a cavernous void rimmed with jagged teeth and exhales diseased breath that can poison a man in seconds.

This sea monster haunts the coasts of the northern British Isles and can bring catastrophe to whole areas, from famine or drought to plague and disease. It is said that its powers are as strong as its hatred of mankind. It lives beneath the waves, where it is invisible, but once it emerges into the air it can be seen and touched. It is a kind of evil sea-centaur, with the body of a man growing from the body of a horse. But instead of appearing strong and magnificent like a centaur, it looks deathly and out of proportion, with long skinny arms and a huge head.

A man named Tammas was out late at night and saw a hideous creature on the coast road, between the sea and a freshwater loch. He knew that running away was the worst thing to do, so he carried on walking towards the nuckelavee, with fear in his heart. As he grew near, the creature reached out his long arms, and Tammas swerved into the loch, splashing fresh water on the horse's legs. The horse reared up, giving Tammas enough time to run across the loch stream and fall safely on the opposite side.

ACTUAL SIZE

WHERE IN THE WORLD?

SCOTLAND

IRELAND

This sea monster comes from Irish legends, but is said to haunt the coasts around Ireland and Scotland, and the islands in between.

DID YOU KNOW?

• The best way to escape from the monster is to run across a freshwater stream, which the nuckelavee hates.

• Only the Sea Mother is more powerful than the nuckelavee. If a person is captured by the demon, he must call out to the Sea Mother for help, and hope that she drags the nuckelavee back into the sea to make him invisible and powerless again.

• The myths go way back in the folklore of the Orcadians, the people of the Orkney Islands, descended from the Vikings and the Picts.

• One of nuckelavee's most hated things is the burning of seaweed to make soda ash, used in household detergents and for making glass. This sends him into a wild rage, and he kills crops and cattle in his anger.

Oni

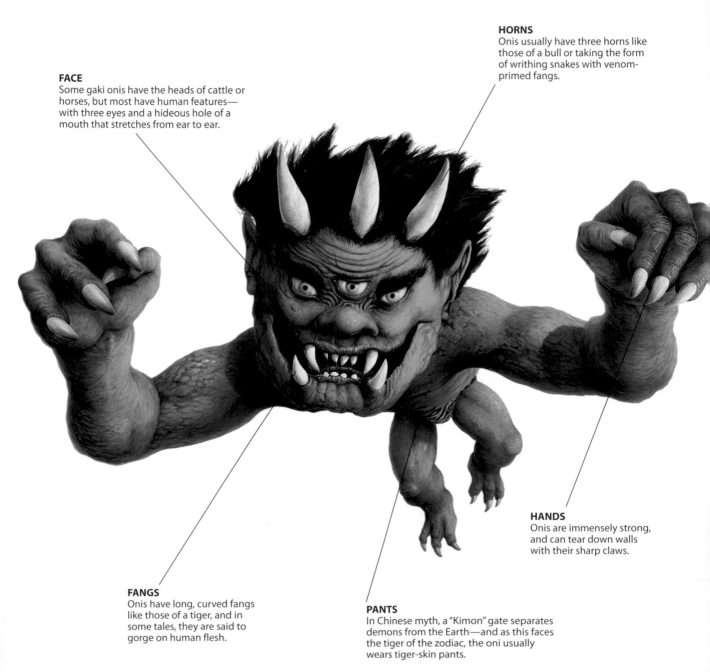

HORNS
Onis usually have three horns like those of a bull or taking the form of writhing snakes with venom-primed fangs.

FACE
Some gaki onis have the heads of cattle or horses, but most have human features—with three eyes and a hideous hole of a mouth that stretches from ear to ear.

HANDS
Onis are immensely strong, and can tear down walls with their sharp claws.

FANGS
Onis have long, curved fangs like those of a tiger, and in some tales, they are said to gorge on human flesh.

PANTS
In Chinese myth, a "Kimon" gate separates demons from the Earth—and as this faces the tiger of the zodiac, the oni usually wears tiger-skin pants.

Whistling gaily as it works, this ghastly creature delights in tormenting the people of Japan, avoiding detection by flitting invisibly through the air or taking human form. Once a Shinto god, it became an evil spirit after Buddhism spread into Japan from China in the 6th century. In earthly guise, it causes disasters, famine, and disease, while its demonic form steals sinners' souls. Many onis have green or red skin. They suffer continual hunger and often have enormous bellies. Hunting down sinners, they take them in a fiery chariot to hell.

The inhabitants of this small Japanese village are blissfully unaware that the extremely dangerous oni is hovering above, waiting to cast its evil spell on them. As it swirls above the village considering what damage it can cause, the residents are getting on with their everyday lives, unaware that their lives are about to be completely transformed. What devastation the oni will bring, nobody knows. Its sheer strength and power could cast a spell causing a terrifying earthquake, a deadly disease, or even a terrible famine.

WHERE IN THE WORLD?

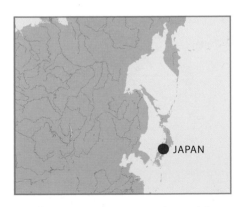

JAPAN

Onis living in the mortal world are found almost exclusively in Japan, although they are thought to have originated in China. Other onis known as gaki inhabit the spirit world or Jigoku (hell) underground.

ACTUAL SIZE

DID YOU KNOW?

• A woman may turn into an oni under the stress of jealousy or grief, while other onis may be the souls of people who died of plague or famine.

• The Buddhist sage Nichiren regarded the onis as a punishment for the sins of the Japanese, so he founded a school to reform people.

• Although female onis take the form of beautiful women, they are prone to violent outbursts of rage.

Peryton

WINGS
The peryton had enormous green feather wings and a green or light blue feather-covered tail and body, like a bird.

HEAD
The head and front legs of this monster were those of a green-colored deer or stag, with giant antlers.

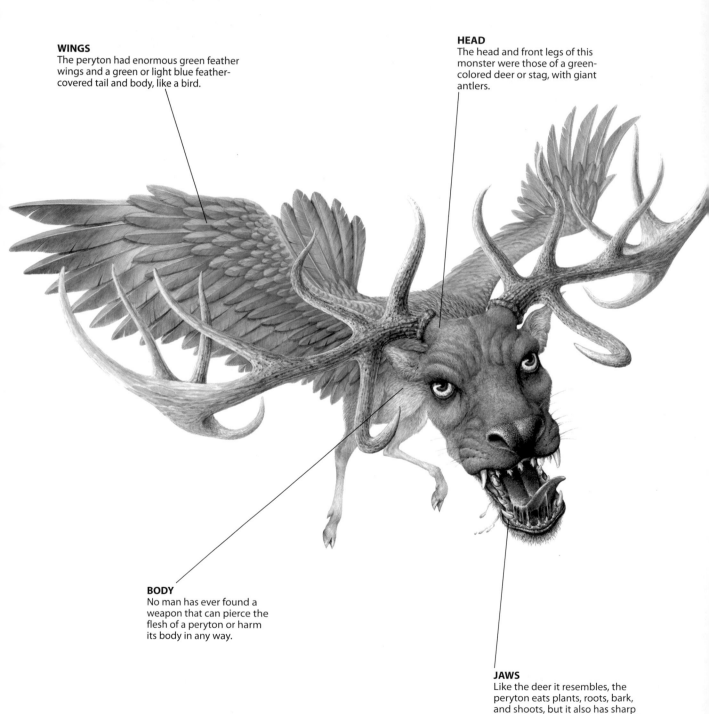

BODY
No man has ever found a weapon that can pierce the flesh of a peryton or harm its body in any way.

JAWS
Like the deer it resembles, the peryton eats plants, roots, bark, and shoots, but it also has sharp teeth for tearing into human flesh.

A peryton is a majestic beast said to attack sailors around the Straits of Gibraltar on their way to and from the Mediterranean. They swoop through the skies on their mighty wings and tend to stick together in large flocks. Strangely, as they fly overhead, the shadow they cast on the ground or ocean surface is the shape of a human. If a peryton killed a person and soaked itself in the half-eaten body, the shadow would take back the peryton's form, and that beast would be unable to kill a human again. A peryton cannot be killed by any known weapon.

A Roman named Scipio and his army invaded the ancient city of Carthage sometime in the second or third century BC. They were attacked by a flock of perytons, which flew at them again and again. Although they could not be killed with the Romans' swords and spears, the army was eventually able to defeat the creatures as each peryton is only able to kill one human. This limited the number of deaths for the Romans and left some of the army still standing.

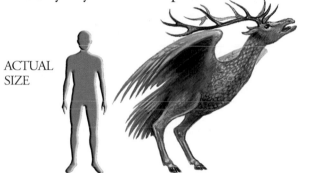

ACTUAL SIZE

WHERE IN THE WORLD?

ATLANTIC OCEAN

● STRAITS OF GIBRALTAR

Although Perytons attacked sailors near Gibraltar, they were said to come from Atlantis, which some believe is lost beneath the Atlantic Ocean.

DID YOU KNOW?

• The peryton's human shadow suggested to believers that the creatures were the trapped souls of humans such as dead sailors or travelers or of murderers imprisoned in a beast's body.

• Once a peryton has killed a man, his soul is said to be put at rest, his shadow returns to its proper form, and the creature can live the rest of its life in peace. Most descriptions of the perytons suggest they are green or blue in color, but in some accounts they are a rainbow of shades, from golden, scarlet, or orange to white, gray, or black.

• When they are not in flight, perytons stick to their forest homes, grazing and resting, as far from humans as they can get.

ANCIENT LEGENDS

Rumpelstiltskin

HEAD
His pointed hat and pointed ears identify Rumpelstiltskin as a dwarf.

HANDS
Rumpelstiltskin's swift hands have the magical ability to spin straw into gold. They can also whip up nightmares to haunt a human's sleep.

ARMS
The dwarf's wiry arms possess superhuman strength, enabling him to tear his own body in half.

FEET
He is a skilled dancer, so his traditional pointed dwarf shoes do not interfere with his dance around his campfire in the woods at night.

A poor miller hoping to impress the king boasts that his daughter can spin straw into gold. The king shuts her in a tower room with nothing but straw and a spinning wheel. She is expected to spin the straw into gold by morning. If she fails, she will be killed. But the young woman cannot spin straw into gold. She begins to despair, and then a dwarf named Rumpelstiltskin appears in the locked room. In exchange for her necklace, the dwarf uses his magical powers to spin the straw into gold. Impressed, the king tells her to do it again and locks her in the tower room with even more straw on the second night.

Rumpelstiltskin appears again, and this time she trades him her ring for spinning the straw into gold for her. The king demands that she repeat the trick a third night and locks her up one last time. Now she has nothing left to trade the dwarf, so she promises her first-born child to him if he will spin the straw into gold. The king marries her. Nothing more is heard of Rumpelstiltskin until she bears her first child and the dwarf comes to claim the baby.

ACTUAL SIZE

WHERE IN THE WORLD?

GERMANY

Rumpelstiltskin is one of the numerous fairy tales collected by the Brothers Grimm in Germany during the early 1800s.

DID YOU KNOW?

• **The young woman offers Rumpelstiltskin all her riches if he will allow her to keep her baby. He agrees that she may keep her child if she can guess his name. He gives her three days for the task. A messenger overhears Rumpelstiltskin singing a rhyme about his name and reports the dwarf's name to the woman.**

• **When she correctly guesses his name, Rumpelstiltskin is enraged. He stomps his right foot so hard that it is buried into the ground up to his waist. In his fury, he grabs his own left foot in both hands and rips himself in two.**

• **Rumpelstiltskin appears in the animated movie *Shrek the Third* as a member of Prince Charming's army of villains.**

Sleipnir

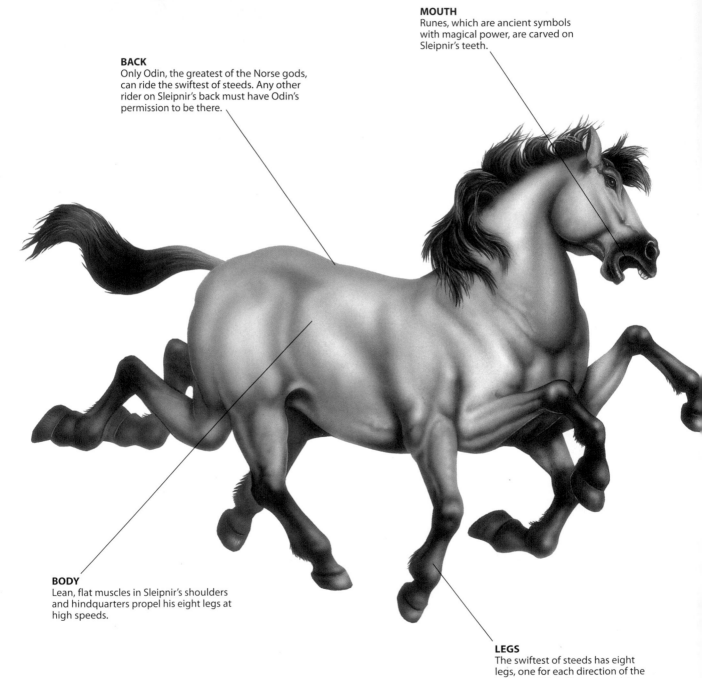

MOUTH
Runes, which are ancient symbols with magical power, are carved on Sleipnir's teeth.

BACK
Only Odin, the greatest of the Norse gods, can ride the swiftest of steeds. Any other rider on Sleipnir's back must have Odin's permission to be there.

BODY
Lean, flat muscles in Sleipnir's shoulders and hindquarters propel his eight legs at high speeds.

LEGS
The swiftest of steeds has eight legs, one for each direction of the compass. His gallop cannot be slowed by water, air, or land.

Sleipnir is Odin's magical eight-legged steed. The greatest of all horses, and the swiftest on Earth, Sleipnir is the offspring of the shape-shifting god Loki and the horse of the giants. Odin, the chief god in Norse mythology, first sees Sleipnir as a colt being led by Loki with a rope. Odin admires the young horse, and Loki gives Sleipnir to him. He is the perfect mount for a god because no horse can keep up with him.

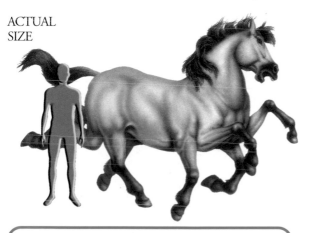

ACTUAL SIZE

Sleipnir can travel anywhere, galloping on top of ocean waves and over rainbows. He can also carry his rider into the land of the dead and back again safely. Odin's son Hermod rides Sleipnir for 9 days and nights through a valley so deep and dark he cannot see a thing. He rides into the realm of the dead to find his dead brother, Balder. Sleipnir leaps over the vast iron gates into the land of the dead. The rotting dead all stare. Hermod strikes a deal with the ruler of the underworld for the return of his brother. If everything in all 9 worlds, dead and alive, will weep for Balder, Hermod may take his brother home.

WHERE IN THE WORLD?

NORWAY

In Norse mythology, Sleipnir may be found near Norway in the land of the gods, the realm of the dead, or anywhere in between.

DID YOU KNOW?

• **Hermod rides Sleipnir out of the land of the dead back to Asgard, the world of the gods. Hermod manages to convince every living and dead creature to weep for his brother Balder, with one exception. A single giantess refuses to cry, so Balder has to remain among the dead.**

• **Odin once rode Sleipnir to the land of the giants, where Odin bet his own head that Sleipnir could outrun any of their horses. Sleipnir easily beat even the fastest of the giants' horses.**

• **The bones of horses are often found in Viking burials. Horses were buried with their owners in the belief that they could carry their owner through the afterlife.**

Snow Spirit

ICICLES
The snow spirit has icicles for fingers, which welcome people into her icy and deathly embrace.

FACE
A snow spirit has the most beautiful and striking face to tempt people into trusting her, but one blast of her breath is enough to blow down a door or blast through a wall.

CLOTHING
Beautifully dressed in shimmering white, the snow spirit wears a floating garment that may be bloodstained on the hem.

FEET
Some stories say that a snow spirit has no feet, and simply floats above the icy ground. Others say that her feet are bloodstained like her clothes.

The snow spirit is as changeable as the weather that makes her. She represents the spirit of the storm but can be beautiful and serene if she chooses. As she travels through the winter nights, she leaves no footprints in the snow. Her icy breath can easily blow down the door of a house, where she may simply kill the people sleeping there or wake them and ask to be invited into their home for shelter. Once she is inside, her presence makes the temperature drop even lower than the stormy night outside. She can freeze a person with a single breath or a touch from her icicle fingers.

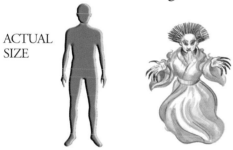

ACTUAL SIZE

A father and his son were sheltering from a snowstorm in the middle of winter. While his father slept by the fire, the son was woken by a sudden drop in temperature. He watched in horror as a snow spirit leaned over his father and turned him to ice. She liked the young man and spared his life, but told him never to tell anyone what he had seen. Years later, sitting with his wife, he broke his word to the snow spirit. His wife turned white and cold, and disappeared into thin air.

WHERE IN THE WORLD?

JAPAN

The snow spirit haunts the snowy mountains of Japan, and in different areas they tell varying tales of what horrors she gets up to.

DID YOU KNOW?

• The traditional snow spirit story has different endings. In one, the son tells his wife how much she reminds him of a snow spirit he once met. His wife—who is the snow spirit—lets him live for the sake of their children but never sees him again.

• In another version of the tale, the son cannot bear to keep the secret from his wife and tells her that he once met a snow spirit. Again, his wife is the snow spirit, but allows him to live as he has told only her, not another mortal person.

• The myth of the snow spirit is sometimes mixed in with that of Yuki-Onna, and instead of raiding people's homes, she appears to lost travelers and tricks them into losing their way, even leading them off the edge of mountains.

Stymphalian Birds

SIZE
The birds are not giants, but are about the size of a heron or crane, with a large wingspan and long, slender legs.

FEATHERS
The plumage of each bird is made up of many hundreds of bronze or iron feathers, each one of them razor sharp.

WASTE
The mess left by these birds is extremely toxic and can easily kill a person.

BEAK
The beak and claws of each bird are also made of metal, strong enough to pierce the flesh of their victims and even to rip through metal armor.

These birds are vicious man-eaters with an arsenal of weapons attached to their body in the form of metal feathers, claws, and beaks. They are as vicious as a lion when they are hungry, and attack unsuspecting victims, swooping out of the sky to satisfy their appetite for flesh. They can shoot their feathers like arrows, to spear the horrified humans down below. Ordinary armor does nothing to stop them, but armor made of cork will trap the bird's beak and keep the wearer safe. They live in vast flocks in the dense, dark forests by the lake, and breed often to increase their numbers.

When Hercules was given the task of getting rid of these birds, he thought it would be easier than his other tasks. However, that wasn't so. He couldn't get the birds out of the trees to shoot at them. The goddess Athena came to his aid. She asked the blacksmith god, Hephaestus, to make a giant pair of noisemaking clappers. Hercules used his amazing strength to bang these clappers together and make such a noise the birds flew from the trees. He shot down hundreds of them, and the rest were frightened away.

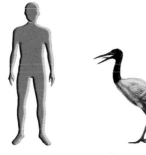

ACTUAL SIZE

WHERE IN THE WORLD?

GREECE

The birds terrorize the people living around Lake Stymphalia in the ancient city of Arcadia, in southern Greece.

DID YOU KNOW?

• **According to one story, the birds were chased to Lake Stymphalia by a pack of wolves. The dark forests were an ideal hiding and roosting place for them to live in safety.**

• **Hercules had a quiver of deadly arrows that he rained into the sky to bring down the birds as they tried to escape. In some pictures, though, he is shown aiming at them with his catapult.**

• **The birds that were not killed by Hercules kept on flying and never returned to Greece. They may have settled on the island of Ares in the Euxine Sea, where they were later seen by Jason and his Argonauts.**

• **As well as killing people, the birds destroyed crops and brought starvation to the land.**

Tengu

FLIGHT
Despite having wings, tengu more often move short distances by disappearing and reappearing somewhere else.

WINGS
Their bird wings may be black like the feathers of a crow or shimmering and colorful like the wings of a hummingbird.

BEAK
Many tengu are shown as part bird, part human, especially around the mouth, which is a cross between a beak and a human face.

TALKING
Tengu do not move their beak or mouthparts when they speak. Their thoughts seem to be projected into the listener's mind, like telepathy.

There are two types of tengu, but the most ancient is the crow tengu with the beak, claws, and feathered body of a bird, but the face and legs of a human. These evil demons get up to all sorts of mischief: misleading holy men, starting fires, and kidnapping and eating children. They can change themselves into the form of a person (although that person will often have a large, hooked nose). A tengu can appear to people in their dreams and can even possess a waking person to use them as a body for talking through. They are also said to love poetry!

On a trip to the mountains, a hunter entered a clearing and saw a snake kill a bird. Soon after, a boar ran into the clearing and ate the snake. The hunter thought he should kill the boar but then changed his mind. He did not want to be the next link in a chain of killing—who knows what might kill him to continue the chain? As he journeyed home, a tengu called to him from the treetops. It told him how wise he had been, for if he had killed the boar, the tengu would have killed him.

ACTUAL SIZE

WHERE IN THE WORLD?

JAPAN

Tengu are linked to the Japanese religions of Shintoism and Buddhism. Shrines with bird-faced statues can be seen around Japan.

DID YOU KNOW?

• The other kind of tengu is a mountain priest with a long, sausage-shaped nose, who may be wicked or kind, sometimes helping lost children find their way home.

• In 1860, the Japanese government wrote to the tengu, asking them to leave their mountain so that the shogun (an important leader) could visit safely.

• Tengu are often shown in Japanese art riding on a boar instead of a horse. Some are shown with arms as well as wings, to hold a weapon.

• Buddhist priests were often plagued by tengu demons, who would show them the error of their ways. The priests were warned that if they got too self-important or corrupt, the tengu would get them, and their noses would become long and beaklike.

Witch

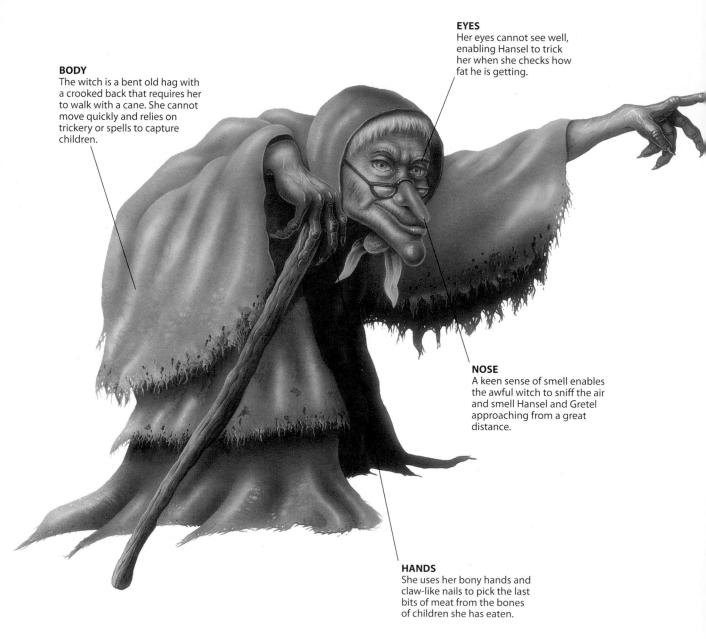

EYES
Her eyes cannot see well, enabling Hansel to trick her when she checks how fat he is getting.

BODY
The witch is a bent old hag with a crooked back that requires her to walk with a cane. She cannot move quickly and relies on trickery or spells to capture children.

NOSE
A keen sense of smell enables the awful witch to sniff the air and smell Hansel and Gretel approaching from a great distance.

HANDS
She uses her bony hands and claw-like nails to pick the last bits of meat from the bones of children she has eaten.

Deep in a forest in southern Germany lives a cannibal witch, who dines on the tender flesh of lost children. Hansel and Gretel, the children of a poor woodcutter, are abandoned deep in the forest when there is not enough food for their family to survive. Hansel cleverly leaves a trail of breadcrumbs when he and his sister are led into the forest, thinking they can follow it back home. However, the birds eat the breadcrumb trail and the children are lost. They find a gingerbread house with sugar windows and a cake roof. The hungry children start to nibble at the house, not knowing it is the home of an evil witch.

The witch invites Hansel and Gretel in for a meal. She imprisons Hansel in a shed and forces Gretel to cook for her brother so that he will fatten up. Hansel eats rich food every day, but Gretel is fed only scraps. The day arrives when the witch is ready to eat Hansel. She fires up her oven and orders Gretel to get in it to test how hot it is. Sensing a trick, Gretel shoves the witch in and slams the door shut on her.

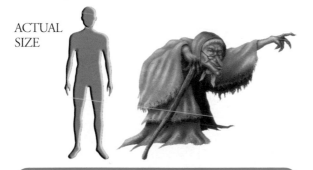

ACTUAL SIZE

WHERE IN THE WORLD?

GERMANY

Hansel and Gretel live on the outskirts of the magical Black Forest in southwestern Germany.

DID YOU KNOW?

• Every day, the nearsighted witch tested how fat Hansel was getting by feeling his finger. Hansel fooled her into thinking he was staying thin by holding out a small chicken bone instead of his finger for her to feel.

• Because of Gretel's quick thinking, the witch is baked in her own oven. Gretel frees Hansel from the shed and they stuff their pockets with jewels from the witch's house. They return to their father's house with the riches, and no one in their family ever goes hungry again.

• An operatic version of the story titled *Hänsel und Gretel* was written by German composer Engelbert Humperdinck (1854–1921) in 1891.

Yama Uba

EYES
Despite her age, her eyes are piercing and full of life and vigor.

MOUTH
The old crone's mouth is said to be as wide as her face, stretching from ear to ear. In some tales, she has a second mouth at the top of her head.

HAIR
She has extremely long, tangled white hair that she can bring to life to reel in her victims.

CLOTHES
Her traditional red kimono may look beautiful from a distance, but up close it is dirty, ragged, and old.

Yama Uba is a ghost who takes the form of a frightening old woman lurking in the Japanese mountains. She seeks out people who are lost and invites them back to her home to help them. She offers food and drink, and a bed for the night—but then pounces on them as they sleep. She has an ax that she sharpens for every new victim and is much feared by the inhabitants of the villages nearby. Yama Uba can turn herself into a beautiful young woman to make her victims feel safe, but many local people have seen her dancing at midnight in her real demonic form.

This evil spirit has different methods of catching her victims. At times, instead of guiding them back to her mountain hut, she turns her hair into snakes. These lively creatures grab her prey and feed it into the mouth near the top of her head. Sometimes, pretending to help the poor lost travelers, she leads them along dangerous mountain paths until they are too weary to walk properly. When they totter and fall to their death, she climbs down and starts to feed on their flesh.

ACTUAL SIZE

WHERE IN THE WORLD?

JAPAN

Yama Uba lurks in the forested areas in the mountains of Japan. Various regions tell tales of her wickedness and magic.

DID YOU KNOW?

• **Her name means "old woman in the mountains" from the Japanese "yama," which means mountain, and "uba," which means old woman or crone. Her name is also spelled Yamanba or Yamamba.**

• **Yama Uba is not fussy about who she eats. She usually captures adults who are traveling alone, but parents often warn their children about the dangers of straying too far from the house in case she whisks them away.**

• **In some Japanese tales, Yama Uba raises a son, called Kintarou, who grows up to become a famous warrior and hero in national folklore.**

• **She is sometimes shown with mountain deer and monkeys alongside her.**

Yuki-Onna

FACE
Her skin is ghostly pale, sometimes even see-through, but her eyes are terrifying and can freeze a human in his tracks with pure fear.

BREATH
Yuki-Onna's breath is as cold as ice, and she can freeze the body of her victim if she can keep him with her for long enough.

HAIR
Yuki-Onna's long, black hair flows in straight torrents down her back, making her even more captivating to look at.

CLOTHES
She sometimes wears a beautiful Japanese kimono, as white as the snowy landscapes she lives in, so that only her hair and face are visible.

42

This Japanese character appears during snowstorms, especially at night. It is said that she is the spirit of a woman who perished during a dreadful storm and has lingered on Earth to get her revenge. She behaves in different ways according to her mood. Some people believe that she was pregnant when she died and is avenging the life of her lost child. She appears in the snow clutching a tiny, wailing baby, and asks for help from travelers. If she can persuade them to take the child from her, the unsuspecting traveler becomes instantly frozen as they touch the crying bundle.

ACTUAL SIZE

Sometimes Yuki-Onna has no baby, but follows lost travelers and offers to guide them through the raging storm. If they are desperate enough to put their trust in her, she leads them off the path to die of exposure to the elements. On other occasions, she talks to lonely souls who are trapped by the storm, seeming to keep them company through the long, bitter night. If they stay in her company for long enough, her icy breath eventually freezes them into a frost-covered corpse.

WHERE IN THE WORLD?

JAPAN

Tales of Yuki-Onna are told throughout Japan but with variations in different parts of the country.

DID YOU KNOW?

• **The most wicked Yuki-Onna uses her icy beauty to trick men into falling in love with her. One kiss from her subzero lips is enough to kill them, and then she drinks their blood like a vampire.**

• **In Japanese, "yuki" means "snow" and "onna" means "woman," making her the "snow woman."**

• **One of the most poetic versions of Yuki-Onna's tale says that she was a princess of the moon who came down to Earth during a snowfall, to take a closer look. However, once she landed she could not return to the sky, for the snow could not carry her back up.**

• **In some parts of Japan, Yuki-Onna only appears on January 15. Others believe she arrives with the New Year and stays through January.**

Baba Yaga
Area: Russia, Eastern Europe
Features: Usually a very old woman; legs bony as a skeleton; hooked nose; eyes that can turn victims into stone

Banshee
Area: Scotland, Ireland
Features: Can be young and beautiful or old and ugly; knotted, long hair; wears a long gray cloak and mourning clothes or a green dress; eyes red from crying; horrifying wail

Black Dog
Area: British Isles, Europe, eastern North America
Features: Blacker-than-night coat; long, sharp teeth; claws on huge paws that don't make a sound when it walks; eyes glow or are empty, black pits

European Unicorns
Area: Britain, France, Germany, Italy
Features: White horse-like animal with a pure white horn on its forehead; blood has magical powers

Evil Queen
Area: Germany
Features: Beautiful, but can change herself into many forms

Fenrir
Area: Scandinavia
Features: Huge wolf; when its mouth is open, the upper jaw reaches the sky and the lower jaw touches the Earth; muscular body; can hear from very far away

Ghoul
Area: Persia, Arabia
Features: Looks like a skeleton covered in skin; sunken eyes and nose; often wears rags; razor-sharp teeth

Huitzilopochtli
Area: Mexico
Features: Aztec god of the sun; painted blue; oversized teeth; wears a headdress of hummingbird feathers

Mordred
Area: Camelot
Features: Wears plate armor and a helmet; his shield is made of wood and covered in leather

Nuckelavee
Area: Ireland, Scotland
Features: The body of a man growing out of a horse; no skin to cover muscle; lives in the sea; eyes lit with fire; the man's head is too large for his body; poisonous breath

Oni

Area: Japan

Features: Human-like face with three eyes and a mouth that stretches from ear to ear; long, curved fangs; three horns; strong hands with claws; usually wears tiger-skin pants

Peryton

Area: Straits of Gibraltar

Features: Half deer, half bird; no weapon can pierce its flesh; giant antlers

Rumpelstiltskin

Area: Germany

Features: Dwarf; hands can spin straw into gold; arms have superhuman strength

Sleipnir

Area: Norway

Features: Eight-legged horse; fastest on Earth; magical symbols carved into its teeth

Snow Spirit

Area: Japan

Features: Beautiful face; breath can blow down a door or freeze a person; fingers are icicles; dresses in shimmering white

Stymphalian Birds

Area: Greece

Features: Bronze or iron feathers that are sharp as razors; the birds' waste is toxic; beak and claws are made of metal

Tengu

Area: Japan

Features: Feathered body of a crow, face and legs of a human; can change into a person; can disappear and reappear somewhere else; wings are black or shimmering; uses telepathy to communicate

Witch

Area: Germany

Features: Hag with a bent back; poor eyesight; good sense of smell; claw-like nails

Yama Uba

Area: Japan

Features: Ghost who looks like an old woman; mouth stretches across her whole face; long, tangled white hair that she uses to reel in victims; wears a red kimono

Yuki-Onna

Area: Japan

Features: Spirit who appears during snowstorms; eyes can freeze someone who looks into them; breath is as cold as ice; sometimes wears a white kimono; long, black hair

Glossary

cannibal: an animal or human who eats its own kind

cartilage: stretchy matter that makes up some of the body

cower: to move away from something in fear

decay: rotting

disguise: a change in looks or clothing that hides who you are

famine: having a very low supply of food

grudge: dislike that lasts a long time

haggard: having a hungry or tired look

immortal: endless life

jostle: to knock against something

keen: very good

loch: a long, narrow body of water which leads to the sea

malice: meanness

medieval: having to do with the Middle Ages

mortal: someone certain to die

mortar: a deep bowl in which medicine or food is crushed

peddler: someone who sells goods

pestle: a tool shaped like a club used for crushing medicine or food

sinews: the matter connecting muscle to bone

sporadic: occasional

subterranean: underground

telepathy: communication that takes place in the mind without speech or signs

For More Information

Books

Bernard, Catherine. *Celtic Mythology*. Berkeley Heights, NJ: Enslow Publishers, 2003.

Grimm, Jacob, Wilhelm Grimm, and Charles Perrault. *Rapunzel and Other Magic Fairytales*. Translated by Anthea Bell. London: Egmont, 2006.

McCaughrean, Geraldine. *The Silver Treasure: Myths and Legends of the World*. New York: M.K. McElderry Books, 1997.

Ozaki, Yei Theodora. *Japanese Fairy Tales*. New York: Cosimo Classics, 2004.

Renison, Jessica. *The Secret History of Unicorns*. London: Kandour Limited., 2007

Yomtov, Nelson. *Jason and the Golden Fleece*. Minneapolis, MN: Stone Arch Books, 2009.

Web Sites

American Folklore
http://americanfolklore.net/folklore/myths-legends
Read more legends known in the United States.

Folk Legends
http://web-japan.org/kidsweb/folk/
Read the folktales of Japan and play games about Japanese culture.

World Myths and Legends in Art
www.artsmia.org/world-myths/
See how myths and legends are used in the art collection at the Minneapolis Institute of Art.

Index